Tree Kangaroos

Julie Murray

Abdo Kids Junior
is an Imprint of Abdo Kids
abdobooks.com

Abdo
INTERESTING ANIMALS
Kids

abdobooks.com

Published by Abdo Kids, a division of ABDO, P.O. Box 398166, Minneapolis, Minnesota 55439.

Printed in the United States of America, North Mankato, Minnesota.

102022

012023

THIS BOOK CONTAINS RECYCLED MATERIALS

Photo Credits: Getty Images, Minden Pictures, Shutterstock

Production Contributors: Teddy Borth, Jennie Forsberg, Grace Hansen

Design Contributors: Candice Keimig, Pakou Moua

Library of Congress Control Number: 2022937178

Publisher's Cataloging-in-Publication Data

Names: Murray, Julie, author.

Title: Tree kangaroos / by Julie Murray

Description: Minneapolis, Minnesota : Abdo Kids, 2023 | Series: Interesting animals | Includes online resources and index.

Identifiers: ISBN 9781098264178 (lib. bdg.) | ISBN 9781098264734 (ebook) | ISBN 9781098265014 (Read-to-Me ebook)

Subjects: LCSH: Tree kangaroos--Juvenile literature. | Marsupials--Juvenile literature. | Animals--Juvenile literature. | Zoology--Juvenile literature.

Classification: DDC 599.22--dc23

Table of Contents

Tree Kangaroos

Tree kangaroos live in Australia and New Guinea. There are 14 different kinds.

Asia
Africa
New Guinea
Australia

All tree kangaroos live in forests. They stay up in trees!

Tree kangaroos have a thick body. They can weigh up to 30 pounds (13.6 kg).

They have short hair. They come in different colors.

They have a long tail.

Their tail helps them

balance.

Tree kangaroos have
strong legs and arms.
They are good climbers.

They are good jumpers too!

They jump from tree to tree.

They eat leaves, flowers, and fruit.

Mothers carry babies in their **pouch**. Babies stay there for seven months.

Tree Kangaroo Features

short hair

lighter underside is common

long tail

strong arms and legs

Glossary

balance
hold steady.

pouch
a natural pocket of skin in some female animals that is used to hold and carry young.

Index